Life in the
STONE AGE

THIS EDITION
Produced for DK by WonderLab Group LLC
Jennifer Emmett, Erica Green, Kate Hale, *Founders*

Editor Maya Myers; **Photography Editor** Kelley Miller; **Managing Editor** Rachel Houghton;
Designers Project Design Company; **Researcher** Michelle Harris; **Copy Editor** Lori Merritt;
Indexer Connie Binder; **Proofreader** Susan K. Hom; **Series Reading Specialist** Dr. Jennifer Albro;
Sensitivity Reader Ebonye Gussine Wilkins; **Content Expert** Deborah Olszewski

First American Edition, 2025
Published in the United States by DK Publishing, a division of Penguin Random House LLC
1745 Broadway, 20th Floor, New York, NY 10019

Copyright © 2025 Dorling Kindersley Limited
25 26 27 10 9 8 7 6 5 4 3 2 1
001–345899–July/2025

All rights reserved.
Without limiting the rights under the copyright reserved above, no part of this publication may be reproduced, stored in or introduced into a retrieval system, or transmitted, in any form, or by any means (electronic, mechanical, photocopying, recording, or otherwise), without the prior written permission of the copyright owner. Published in Great Britain by Dorling Kindersley Limited

A catalog record for this book is available from the Library of Congress.
HC ISBN: 978-0-5939-6647-1
PB ISBN: 978-0-5939-6646-4

DK books are available at special discounts when purchased in bulk for sales promotions, premiums, fund-raising, or educational use. For details, contact:
DK Publishing Special Markets, 1745 Broadway, 20th Floor, New York, NY 10019
SpecialSales@dk.com

Printed and bound in China
Super Readers Lexile® levels 500L to 610L
Lexile® is the registered trademark of MetaMetrics, Inc. Copyright © 2024 MetaMetrics, Inc. All rights reserved.

The publisher would like to thank the following for their kind permission to reproduce their images:
a=above; c=center; b=below; l=left; r=right; t=top; b/g=background

123RF.com: Guillermo Avello; Gleb Semenov 11b, Raldi Somers 14cl, PaylessImages 21cl, 21cr, 21tr, Adwo123 24bl, 24t, Arindam Banerjee 28–29 b/g; **Dorling Kindersley:** Royal Pavilion & Museums, Brighton & Hove 7tr, 7br, Pitt Rivers Museum, University of Oxford 16cl, Royal Pavilion & Museums, Brighton & Hove 6cr; **Dreamstime.com:** Goldilock Project 4–5, Aleksei Gorodenkov 3, David Head 14–15, Jacques Jacobsz 12bl, Isselee 14bl, Alanjeffery 19b, Lorna 26tl; **Getty Images:** Universal History Archive 24tr, De Agostini / Dea / G. Dagli Orti 25bl, Universal Images Group / Universal History Archive 25tr; **Getty Images / iStock:** Mark Devereux 26–27, Ibrahim Halil Yapici 1; **iStockphoto.com:** Kdgeisler 8–9 b/g; **Klint Janulis:** 22tr, 22bl, 22bc, 23b/g; **Science Photo Library:** S. Entressangle / E. Daynes 13tr, 22c; **Shutterstock.com:** Daumantas Liekis 13tl

Cover images: *Front:* **Dreamstime.com:** Alain Lacroix; **Getty Images / iStock:** Pavel Naumov t;
Back: **Dreamstime.com:** Alona Zhitnaya cr; **Getty Images / iStock:** Pavel Naumov cl

All other images © Dorling Kindersley
www.dk.com

Publisher's note: Stone Age scenes shown in photographs have been posed with models based on current understanding of Stone Age culture and practices from around the world.

Level 2

Life in the STONE AGE

Deborah Lock

Contents

6	The Stone Age
8	Staying Warm
14	On the Hunt
20	Using Plants
24	Early Culture

28 What Came Next?
30 Glossary
31 Index
32 Quiz

The Stone Age

The Stone Age is the time when the first people lived. It's divided into three periods. Different names for the periods may be used in different parts of the world.

Old Stone Age: *from 3.3 million to around 25,000 years ago*

People made rough stone tools for hunting and cutting meat and plants.

Middle Stone Age: *from around 25,000 to as recently as 6,500 years ago*

People made new tools such as harpoon tips from deer antlers.

New Stone Age: *from between 11,000 and 6,500 years ago to 4,000 years ago*

People became farmers. Farming began at different times in different parts of the world.

People still used tools made from stone. Some tools, such as axes, were smoothed and polished.

Staying Warm

Ice covered parts of the world at times during the Stone Age. Early people had to find ways to survive the cold.

People moved their camps each season. They gathered plants and hunted animals.

Animals such as deer moved from place to place to find food. People followed animals so that they could hunt them.

Replica of a Stone Age shelter

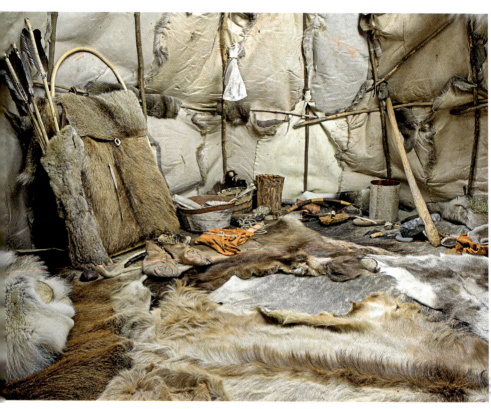

Animal skins covered the floor to keep the inside warm.

People needed shelters to live in. They made frames from thin tree branches. These were covered in animal skins, grass, or tree bark. This kept the inside of the shelters warm and dry.

In the New Stone Age, people more often used rocks to build homes. This house would have had a woven grass roof. Rainwater ran down the grasses and the inside stayed dry.

Skara Brae, Orkney Islands, Scotland

Early people learned how to make fire. They rubbed pieces of wood together very fast. This created enough heat to catch dried grass and small dry sticks on fire.

People used the fire to cook food and keep warm. Fire also helped keep people safe. Wild animals were scared of fire and stayed away.

People made clothes to stay warm. They softened deerskin to make leather. They used the leather to make tunics and pants. Fur tunics kept them warm during the winter. They filled fur shoes with dried grass for extra warmth.

On the Hunt

Early people hunted all sorts of animals. They caught fish and other animals in rivers and oceans. They trapped birds. They hunted big animals such as boars and deer.

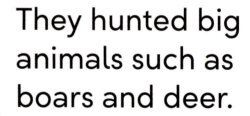
frog

ptarmigan

boar

People used every part of an animal. They hunted small animals such as frogs and hares. They ate the meat. They used the fur and skins to make clothing and shelter. They made tusks and bones into tools.

deer

brown hare

People needed tools for hunting and for making things. They used rock hammers to make tools out of wood, stone, bone, antlers, and shells.

A **pebble hammer** helped to break and shape stone.

People used **flint blades** to cut plants and remove skins from animals.

Hand axes were used to cut meat.

Large land animals such as mammoths were dangerous to hunt. Stone Age hunters learned to throw long spears from very far away. Spears were made from wood and had stone or antler tips. The tips had sharp points to cut through animal skin.

Stone Age people caught and fed wolf cubs. These tamed wolves were the ancestors of the first dogs. They helped people hunt. The dogs also guarded people's camps. They kept away dangerous wild animals such as bears.

Using Plants

Stone Age people did not eat only meat. They gathered plants, fruits, nuts, and roots. People learned which plants were good to eat and which ones would make them sick.

blackberries

hazelnuts

radishes

burdock roots

nettle leaves

willow bark

People also used plants to stay healthy. They soaked burdock roots in hot water to make warm drinks. They added nettle leaves to soups. Willow bark helped to relieve pain.

People used bark from trees to make buckets. They used these buckets to carry and store food and water. They wove flexible branches into baskets to trap fish.

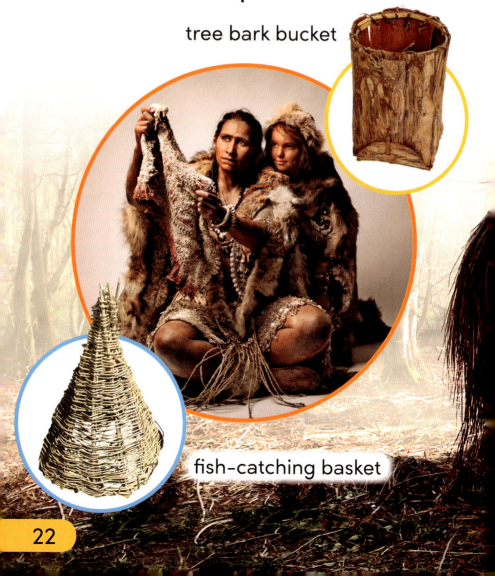

tree bark bucket

fish-catching basket

Early people made rope from thin, strong plant stems. They used the rope to make traps and sew clothes.

Plant rope could be used to tie pieces of wood together, as in this ladder.

Early Culture

These hand paintings are in Argentina.

Early people used caves as shelters and as meeting places. They painted pictures on the walls. They used red, yellow, and brown colors found in soil and soft stones. The black color came from burned wood, called charcoal.

People drew the animals that they hunted on the cave walls. They may have been asking the animal spirits for good luck when hunting.

These cave paintings are in France.

Some Stone Age people believed in good and bad spirits. Shamans were leaders and healers. People believed shamans were connected with the spirit world.

Carved reindeer horn from the Old Stone Age, found in France

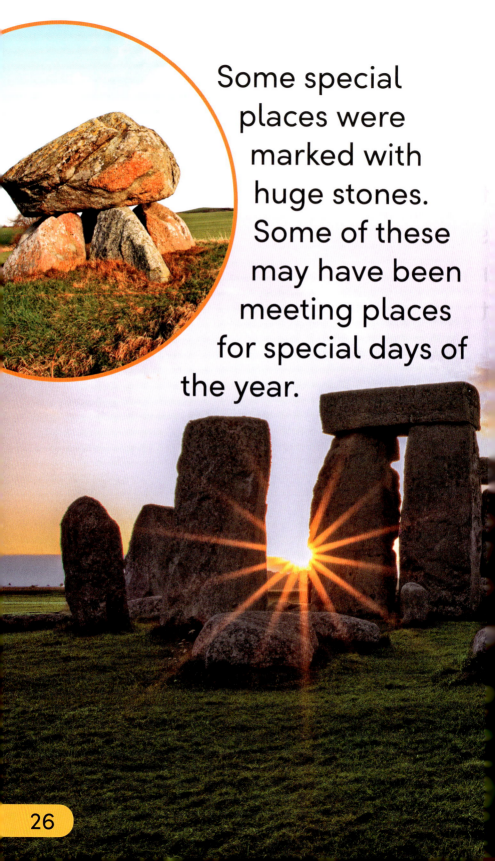

Some special places were marked with huge stones. Some of these may have been meeting places for special days of the year.

Many giant stones are arranged at a site called Stonehenge. The stones allow the rising and setting sun to shine through. Lots of people may have gathered here on the shortest day of the year.

What Came Next?

In the New Stone Age, people stopped moving to follow animals. They lived on small farms. Now, they could raise animals and grow crops.

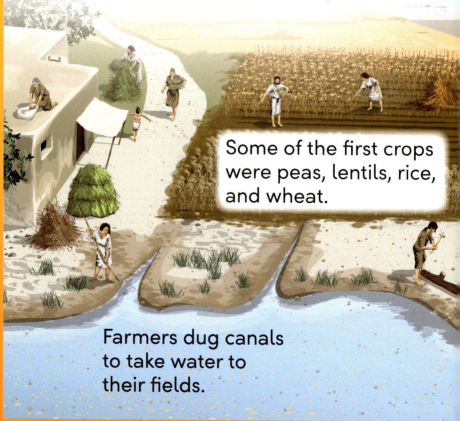

Some of the first crops were peas, lentils, rice, and wheat.

Farmers dug canals to take water to their fields.

Places where people settled together would grow into towns and then cities.

People kept animals for food throughout the year.

Glossary

Charcoal
Burned and blackened wood

Harpoon
A spear with a barbed end used for hunting fish and whales

Mammoth
An extinct large mammal in the elephant family

Middle Stone Age
The period, from around 25,000 to as recently as 6,500 years ago

New Stone Age
The period, from between 11,000 and 6,500 years ago to 4,000 years ago

Old Stone Age
The period, from 3.3 million to around 25,000 years ago

Shaman
A healer and leader in early cultures, thought to be connected to the spirit world

Shelter
A place that keeps people safe and warm

Stone Age
The time when people first lived

Survive
To live despite challenging circumstances

Tool
An object used to perform a task

Tunic
A long, loose-fitting shirt

Tusk
A long tooth that sticks out of an animal's mouth

Index

antler tools 7, 16, 18

axes 7, 16, 17

baskets 22

boars 14

buckets 22

cave paintings 24–25

charcoal 24

clothes 13, 15

deer 7, 9, 13, 14, 15

farming 7, 28

fire 12

fishing 14, 17, 22

frogs 14, 15

harpoons 7, 17

hunting 6, 8, 9, 14–19, 25

mammoths 18

Middle Stone Age 7

New Stone Age 7, 11

Old Stone Age 6, 25

plants 17, 20–23

rope 23

shamans 25

shelters 9, 10–11, 15, 24

spears 17, 18

Stonehenge 27

tools 6, 7, 15–16

wolves 19

Quiz

Answer the questions to see what you have learned. Check your answers in the key below.

1. In which part of the Stone Age did farming begin?
2. Why did Stone Age people follow animals?
3. What was a harpoon used for?
4. What did the black in cave paintings come from?
5. True or False: Stonehenge is made of many giant tree trunks.

1. Neolithic, or New Stone Age 2. So they could hunt them 3. Fishing 4. Charcoal 5. False